Greeting the End of Time

Greeting the End of Time

RAYMOND OLIVER

RESOURCE *Publications* · Eugene, Oregon

GREETING THE END OF TIME

Copyright © 2020 Raymond Oliver. All rights reserved. Except for brief quotations in critical publications or reviews, no part of this book may be reproduced in any manner without prior written permission from the publisher. Write: Permissions, Wipf and Stock Publishers, 199 W. 8th Ave., Suite 3, Eugene, OR 97401.

Resource Publications
An Imprint of Wipf and Stock Publishers
199 W. 8th Ave., Suite 3
Eugene, OR 97401

www.wipfandstock.com

PAPERBACK ISBN: 978-1-7252-7875-2
HARDCOVER ISBN: 978-1-7252-7876-9
EBOOK ISBN: 978-1-7252-7877-6

Manufactured in the U.S.A. • JUNE 29, 2020

to Mary Anne, my help in all these

Contents

Acknowledgements • xiii

Last Visit • 1
Fourteenth Century Fresco, St. Pierre, Brançion • 1
Praying for Forgiveness • 1
Looking Back • 2
The Resurrection of the Body • 2
Resurrection Day in New England • 2
Some Immortality • 3
A Kind of Ongoing Resurrection • 3
Heaven • 4
"all that is made" • 4
The Poet in the Stone Tower • 4
With Thanks to James Lee Burke • 5
Living Forever and Eternal Life • 5
From the Farthest Object • 6
Persistent Searchers • 6
Absolute Zero • 6
The Logos • 7
Meaning • 7
Situations • 8
  Peter Speaks • 8
  Epitaph for a Vitalist • 8

The Universe as Mental Construct • 8
The Compass • 8
Mistaken Identity • 9
God is the Place • 9
A Thanksgiving • 9
Incommensurate • 10
For Eugene Walter • 10
Divine Omniscience Taken Seriously? (Literally) • 10
God • 11
Two Ways • 11
About God • 12
Ancestral • 12
How to Cope • 13
A Bargain • 13
Like a Weakened Immune System • 13
Good vs. Evil • 14
Canonization • 14
How Bizarre • 15
Christendom • 15
One Gist of Christianity • 16
Jesuit Graveyard, Spring Hill College. Ash Wednesday • 16
Eduardus Moody, SJ • 17
For Wil Mills, 1969-2011 • 18
"Rien ne peut nous séparer de l'amour de Dieu" • 18
Two Styles, Two Attitudes • 19
True Dread • 19
August, 2015 • 20
Are • 20
Thinking My Own Death • 21
Afterwards • 21
Seventeenth-Century Gravestone for a Child • 21

Antoine • 22
Alzheimer's • 22
Confrontation • 22
The Record • 23
To Andrei Rublev • 23
Original Stained Glass, North Transept, Reims Cathedral • 23
Notre-Dame de Paris on TV • 24
A Glass of Benedictine, D.O.M. • 24
Going to Aix, Derailed by Taizé • 24
Taizé. Supper at the Reception • 25
Taizé. The Main Church • 25
Beautiful Liturgy, Beautiful Church • 26
The Life of Prayer • 26
Prayer for Continuing Vocation • 27
A Prayer for Fat Souls • 27
For Francis Jammes • 27
Epigrams • 28
The Incarnation • 30
Not the Frontal View • 30
Good Friday. Thinking of Whit • 31
The Burial of Christ: from the Sterzingen Altarpiece • 31
A Question • 32
Weight • 32
Witness • 33
In All Saints Chapel, Sewanee • 33
The Guest • 33
The Jesus Prayer • 34
Poor Woman • 34
Worn Thin, and Pierced • 35
Breakthrough • 35
Four Kinds of Celebration • 36

Lyric at Dawn • 36
Photograph of Manhattan, Winter 1887 • 37
Even As I Walked • 37
In the Medieval Galleries • 37
Recipe • 37
Churchbells Near Laramie, Long Ago • 38
Church Downtown • 39
In an Old Cloistered Library • 39
Across from the De Young Museum • 40
On Hartmut Thieme's Discovery • 40
Medieval, and Renaissance Too • 40
Resonance • 41
The Killing of St. Thomas Becket • 41
Fashions, 1000-2000 AD • 41
Randomness • 42
The Dogmatist • 42
That Old-Time Religion • 43
Surviving Jehovah • 43
Auctions • 43
The Terror • 44
A Vision of Heaven in the U.S. • 45
Jeremiad for St. Jerome • 45
Little New England Essay in Roughly Metrical Prose • 46
Faith, Hope, and Charity • 46
Eden and After • 47
Scripture Lesson • 47
The Trinity, Especially the Holy Spirit • 48
Triads • 48
Figurines in a Sunday School Sandbox • 52
Membership • 52
Baptism at Twelve • 52

A Collegiate Leavetaking • 53
At the Wide Gate • 54
Christian Heritage • 54
Radical Delight • 54
Confirmation • 55
On the Right Surface • 55
Sunday • 56
Anyday Drama • 56
The Little Things • 57
Prayer for Himself • 57
The Indwelling Spirit • 58
"Credo Quia Absurdum" • 58
August 16, Church of the Reconciliation, Taizé • 59
True Desire • 59
A Wedding • 60
Afterlife for a Couple: Two Takes • 60
Compline • 61
Halloween by San Francisco Bay • 61
Christmas Eve • 62
Outside Benson, Arizona • 62
Christmas • 62
New Year's Eve, and the Millennium's • 63
Easter Vigil at St. Mark's • 63

Acknowledgements

Some of these poems and epigrams have appeared in chapbooks (Entries, Fireflies In an Old Yard, Other Times, Private Stock), anthologies (Bread of Life: Contemporary Christian Poetry, A Garland for John Finlay, Odd Angles of Heaven, Order In Variety), one previous collection (Raymond Oliver His Book Of Hours), one newspaper (Berkeley Times), and the following literary journals: Chicago Review, The Compass, The Epigrammatist, The Greensboro Review, Iowa Review, Mississippi Review, Modern Age, Negative Capability, The Neovictorian/Cochlea, Novy Život [in Czech translation], Occident, Perspectives, Prairie Schooner, Sequoia, Southern Humanities Review, The Southern Review, Studia Mystica, and Triquarterly.

Last Visit

Aunt Mamie was a scandal,
All hollowed out with cancer
Like a guttering candle,
With soot-black hairs on sallow
Flesh as collapsed as tallow.
She was no kind of answer
For others on the way;
Except for one odd smile
At last, as if to say
"I'll see you in a while".

Fourteenth Century Fresco, St. Pierre, Brançion

It's Resurrection Day
Six hundred years ago!
Look at the little men,
Women, and children climb
From tombs as from a bath,
Naked from head to toe,
With bodies back again
And smiles to cheer God's wrath.
Is there a better way
To greet the end of time?

Praying for Forgiveness

It's not like placing in a garbage-bin,
Daily, your face, to savor the stench of sin;
It's like a sickly person looking in
The mirror, hoping all the bad signs there
Don't justify his quavers of despair.

Looking Back

If I will ever
be looking back from beyond,
not
as if from a future
but from an otherwhere,
even merely
the sound of car-wheels
crunching gravel
will be freighted with
an almost desperate
nostalgia.

The Resurrection of the Body

Dying's unmaking of the body
Till it, in all its antic, gaudy,
Hateful or lovely incarnations,
Passes beyond our explications
As music exceeds the keys and hands
That make it. No one understands;
But some have faith that One will hear
Our music with a perfect ear.

Resurrection Day in New England

This liquid gleam – sunlight on rainy slate –
Releases life in the grey of graveyard stones
That hints at sweaty birth below, at bones
In labor, on the Day, changing their state.

Some Immortality

I've had some immortality:
The time in which I didn't die,
And never will – all time till now
That I can hold to my mental eye,
All as solid as yesterday
When we took down the Christmas-tree,
Unwinding spiral strings of lights,
You passing ornaments to me
Like baby birds to set in their nests;
A day where morning spread to noon,
Expanding in the warmth of coffee,
And evening couldn't come too soon
With leisurely rain and Raymond Chandler,
And urgent love, our bodies live
And lithe . . . more than forty years
Of life that death cannot contrive
To touch. It makes me want an endless
Line of living moments, connected
With others', and safe between two moments
The point where death had intersected.

A Kind of Ongoing Resurrection

We're a collection, an anthology,
Of memories ending one moment ago.
Now and the past are real; the future, no.
A going-on-ness, like a radio:
That's "now". You hear its fizz? And smell, taste, see?
Multisensual radio – alive!
I feel inserted in this fizz we're in,
Touching it – what a wonder is the skin,
Fingers, and all the rest! – as I begin,
Consciously now, to feel nowness arrive.

Heaven

It's very much like this:
walking down Lincoln Street,
my palmy lane to the Bay,
enjoying joy. Except
that nothing can go wrong.

"all that is made"

Tennyson tried to understand
A flower in a crannied wall;
Blake envisioned a grain of sand;
But Julian hefted in her hand
A hazel-nut, and that was all.

The Poet in the Stone Tower

>   for Friedrich Hölderlin

"I find myself in a medieval tower,
Whose windows two feet deep admit the twitter,
Thus presence, of the birds, for whom this hour
Might be in any of the years that litter
Mere time. Between the tower and the birds,
Then, is complicity: the stone and song
Enfold me quite. For I, both flesh and words,
Find myself equally in tower – strong
But made with time, which claims it as debris –
And birds, which sing out of eternity."

With Thanks to James Lee Burke

and Hackberry Holland

If it's our life experience –
nothing more – we carry
into eternity, it's nice
to know we have no
Ph.D. exam, on being alive,
to pass.
That would all be
in the head; experience of life
seeps through pores and
makes itself known in toes
and genitals and nose and scalp and all,
often itching or dripping.
It's like a many-
dimensioned carnival-ride,
but slow, and long, from birth
to finish.
And we, or someone within,
present it
as entrance-ticket
into eternity.

Living Forever and Eternal Life

At most my stomach holds Thanksgiving dinner,
Not supper too, much less a week of meals.
Memory's like that. It holds my life, and feels
The fuller as I age – though also thinner.
It couldn't hold that much again, much less
Ten centuries-worth of life. So why this need
To live forever – thinning? But compress,
Reduce the gist of life as if to a seed

That's all, an instant ever flowing, and we,
The dead, within it? Yes: eternity.

From the Farthest Object

To get here, light takes fifteen billion years.
Frissons, glissandos of the infinite!
Numbers tickle our keys, and let us hear
The chimes our reason rings, from where it sits.

And yet it is the One we want, or would
If we could pick its pure tone from the whirl
Of static pressing through our brains and blood.
Its music, heard, could harmonize the world.

It is a simple thing, near kin to folly;
Such as loving another person wholly.

Persistent Searchers

The Great Beyond, before our life and after,
Is as beyond us as the grasp of Hamlet
To ants. But we keep grasping, and the laughter
Of critics (gods? they act like gods) distracts us
But cannot shame us from the task at hand –
Harden our fists to beat against the gate
That bars our knowledge of the Mystery Land,
Our origin and destination, our place.

Absolute Zero

None can imagine nothingness.
Not Heideggerian *Nichts*, which rings

With darkness, but lack of anything –
Including mind, with which we press
The void, in our imagining.

The Logos

So dense with meaning that his thoughts take flesh,
God is meaning. We are his words; we mesh
With God as intimately as word with thought.
He will recall us from oblivion,
Remembering all that history had forgot,
Putting together what he'd said and done.

Meaning

Is meaning
something we invent
like a better
can-opener, or
something we find, like a
box of chocolates under
the Christmas tree?

See what sprouts from
a Latin root,
invenire:
"to invent/to find".
Should we
mind this? Just
a matter of the mind?

Situations

Peter Speaks

"Ah, to ignore him truly, like a name
I hadn't heard – not to choose death, or shame!"

Epitaph for a Vitalist

So "Life" is still your guide,
Your standard for all worth –
A life bound to this earth;
As though you hadn't died.

The Universe as Mental Construct

Let's say, at last the number of the beast
Comes up, and with it the eternal yes
To deadness: all intelligence is banished,
No mind is left in which the world exists.
The world alone, stripped to itself, persists.
Or does it? Will it not have likewise vanished
To less than shadows of a vacuum, less
Than echoes of a cry that no one released?

The Compass

During the search for God, as I disjoint
My thoughts and feelings, twisting to see, to find,
I sense that back of the radars of my mind
A needle spins, hovers, trying to point.

Mistaken Identity

I have your interests, God, at heart; you're safe
With me. They can't, in truth, discover you
To be the killer of the innocent –
Indeed, of all of us . . . But if you do
(And I observe you) with your curses strafe
The world – you're Satan. God's the God I meant.

God is the Place

God is the place where we're to be
Remembered. Pray, "Remember me.
And help me let the Good News ring,
So I'll be worth remembering."

A Thanksgiving

God, I've accused you long enough.
Being Creator with such stuff
As water, fire, earth, and air
Would drive the best of us to despair,
At times. Especially this meat
You made us of – something to eat,
As well as live in! What a joke.
You must have thought so, when the smoke
Of offered cows or people rose,
Hopefully, way up to your nose.

Our flesh must die and rot with sin,
Accident, sickness – that's built in,
Just as a ball, tossed up, must fall.
What fun's an ever rising ball?
Worse than tennis without a net.

It's by the rules that you have set,
Like making night to limit day,
That we and you can rightly play.

So thanks for making us from nothing,
Complete with protoplasm stuffing.

Incommensurate

This Groucho Marx of theologians
Won't have a God that fits the mind
Of such as him (that's humankind):
You don't contain solar explosions
In boxes one of us designed.

For Eugene Walter

That "cosmos" is the Greek for "ornament"
Confirms that hyperbolic curve, your bent
Of mind: Imagine – the whole thing's just for fun,
A game for God with stars and moon and sun!
So you, our Harpo Marx, saw tragedy
As sad penultimate, frivolity
As of the essence; and that to imitate
This God, you party! and a fig for Fate.

Divine Omniscience Taken Seriously? (Literally)

"Here is an instance of what God must know:
I used how many toilet-paper squares
When I was six, and stumbled on which stairs?
And what – completely! – did I think, and say,

And do, on every long-since wiped-out day?
Now take this to the trillionth power or so,
Since all that's once been done, or thought, or said,
Or *felt*, is entered in the great GodHead.
And what, for such a chore, does he have to show?"

There is, to seize this truth, some better way.

God

Each language, as if on its own, conceives
Of God, with help of everyone who speaks.
This God is like a fire: just as bright
However lit, by match or lightning-strike.
When "God" the word lights up in human minds,
It's God indeed; no need to search and find,
Just recognize. And do not be dismayed
By forms the fire takes, its many ways
Of burning. It can make you live, or die.
It can be hated, loved, ignored, denied.
You choose. It's there, like the light in your eyes.

Two Ways

For all those centuries, they thought their faith
Strictly provable and compulsory,
A perfect elevator all were forced
Into, that took them up to where they see
God. But the mechanism faltered. Now,
We're shown a flight of stairs, so we can rise
To the occasion, which will be a meeting.
This way's surprising, and good exercise.

About God

Where speculation quits, God is beyond.
Once, God in thunder was the end of thought;
Then, protons knotted tight in nuclear bond . . .

Untie as we may, we'll find no final knot.

Ancestral

Special devotion to the Holy Ghost
Has birthmarked all Azoreans, or most;
Has tinted, even colored their descendents,
Like me. I feel at times its firm resplendence,
As if of Someone just behind my back
I can't twist fast enough to glimpse; whose track,
Though, goes along my solar plexus, leaping
Up to my eyes, where it can show as weeping.
The energy that powers these events –
Not thinking, not emotion – is immense
And quiet like a motion felt within,
Like breath. It's not that "still, small voice" (too thin,
Too verbal). It's a force that's occupied –
Planting its flag for me to see – all pride,
All exaltation of my self and will.
It is not I; it's neither small nor still;
Not conscience.   She has chosen me to choose her,
This Holy Spirit, and I cannot lose her –
Merely ignore or hurt. And when I've died,
She'll bear my print on her to where reside
The others, where transfigured we will all abide.

How to Cope

I know he's waiting there,
Ready to use my mind
To tell me "jump!" from a height,
And worse. – The Prince of the Air,
Though strong, can only bind
His victims in their night,
When they are unaware.
I'm on to him. I say
To every urging, "Here's
The devil," and he's gone
Like dark when light's turned on,
Leaving the stink of fears
To wash – once more – away.

A Bargain

Satan is both convenient fiction
And inconvenient fiend on mission,
Like thunder heard as vicious anger
Of gods, which makes us flee the danger
Of real lightning. We get the two
For the price of one. No need to choose.

Like a Weakened Immune System

No one to love you. So you wail,
Deep in, and all defenses fail
Against the least assault. Despair
Whispers, "for you, there's no one there".

Good vs. Evil

It only takes a sudden
twist of the will like twist
of wire to do madness
and evil: "spontaneous me"
can cut a throat,
crash into oncoming car, leap
across the rail down to street or river . . .
but doing good, aside from acts like dropping
cash into outstretched cup,
is more like through the years becoming
a climate touching with its goodness
humans and beasts and trees and all.
It's steadily moving forward a massive,
carefully shaped being. Unlike
sudden smashing.

Canonization

I've never wanted
to be a saint, covered
with running holy sores, apologizing
for being alive and human.
And yet
there must be a place, even
a name, for those with a
calm unmoving center, people
helpful to others as to
themselves and who
try to abide in that center.
Call them saints, I
don't mind. Might
have met a few. Liked them, even.

How Bizarre

You feel yourself uniquely dear; you are;
You are the Regent Diamond. How bizarre
To know and try to comprehend that each
Human is that Diamond – which are as many,
Therefore, as the grains of sand on a beach.

Christendom

Look at this gallimaufry – hurdygurdy –
Cuckoo clock with the Holy Ghost as birdie –
Empire stoked by aged "eunuchs of God",
Where whips of flagellants and Aaron's rod
Go whirling through the fiery air, to lash
Sparks of the holy from the pyre's ash –
TV evangelist with neon grin
That flashes at the touch of cash and sin –
Maker of Saints Teresa (God's own bride)
And Charlemagne (patron of genocide) –
Crusade, that smorgasbord of death and loot,
Served with a compote of forbidden fruit –
The Sunday service station of the gloss,
Dispensing sermon-gas with hymnal sauce,
The risen Easter Bunny as wonderbread:
All this the Christian bears on heart and head,
Like Atlas with a lurching, screeching load,
Laboring up the pilgrim's Heaven Road.
Only its mother, or its child, could love it.
Easy to say, with show of reason: shove it.
But if you're sick from Dachau, melanoma,
The Universal Darkness, its aroma

Of death and nothing, corpse the final clown –
This is the only medicine-show in town.
So let me shove my scrupulous distress
Up some grotto, and I'll say yes, oh yes.

One Gist of Christianity

All the glorious Old
Testament talk and poetry
of God and his creation (notably
ourselves) – we wouldn't want all that
destroyed, killed, annihilated,
nothinged (notably not
ourselves). And all
the OT feeds the New, with Jesus
leading. He wants to give us
eternal life; we want it
too; they said
he rose from the dead;
his followers will settle
for nothing less.
So, no matter how
you slice it, hack it, chop it, here's
what we want: *death*
must not
have the last word.
We insist.

Jesuit Graveyard, Spring Hill College. Ash Wednesday

Neither abandoned meadow, nor as neat
As golfcourse-cemeteries where defeat

Is marked by fond inscriptions, soft on hard,
Sweet sculpture for the dead – this is a yard
Behind a college, kept in decent form,
With random pine-trees counterpointing the norm
Of ordered stone. The graves are spaced by rows
Of crosses; at the bases dark clay shows
Against the white of marble, but higher up
Their names and years are deep and cleanly cut,
As if on tablets in the Book of Life.
Transfigured death is bright, not dark; no wife,
No child has mourned these men, and when they died
They triumphed, in a last defeat of pride.
This is their field. Foraging robins scatter
The dust, to litanies of squirrel-chatter.

Eduardus Moody, SJ

    Spring Hill College. R.I.P.

You had no excess flesh, or words, or time;
You fused all three with faith as firm as the cross
Around your neck – Jesus in death, a sign
Of life so dense it has no room for loss.

You died at night, still young. Now, in this field,
Years later, I find your Latin name cut deep
On a cross – as if your life were here revealed,
Condensed in stone. Dissolving minerals seep

Toward root-hairs where your flesh, rendered to clay,
Disperses; just as earth mutes an explosion,
So it absorbs the shock of your decay.
No earth, no years will mute the Word you'd chosen.

For Wil Mills, 1969-2011

It's been six years now
since you disappeared, you
on your paths of eternity
where years are nothing and *now*
is all.
      I see you in your family's
living room, weak as a tinkertoy
of matchsticks but for
your will of steel, showing us –
master carpenter, as master
of so many arts you were! – how
to rub oil into your
coffin, handmade by your
cousin and closest friend.
You've had your family carve
into its lid a bit
of German verse I'd taught you:
O Stern und Blume, Geist und Kleid,
Lieb', Leid, und Zeit, und Ewigkeit!
And Englished into your coffin
– our farewell, dear Wil –
O star and flower, spirit and flesh,
Love, pain, and time, and eternity!

"Rien ne peut nous séparer de l'amour de Dieu"

After the Wall Street bombing,
September 1920,
some photographer caught –
as well as carnage and wreckage, body-
parts and hastily draped
bodies with shoes protruding,
and cars overturned

and tangled steel – caught
a multitude of upturned
faces, mostly men, mostly
with caps and moustaches, faces
emptied of dailyness and cleared
for horror.
And no one currently
alive can identify
any
of those faces as anonymous
as pennies.

Yet Frère Roger
could say that "nothing
can separate us from the love of God."

Two Styles, Two Attitudes

Brother Roger's cross at Taizé
Is slabs of glinting wood – a stay,
Sturdy though brief, against decay;
Truer than tombs of those who pay
For stone to last till Judgement Day.

True Dread

Let's say, at death our bodies instantly
(And like our persons, wholly) disappear.
No graveyards, rotting corpses . . . the industry
Of death, that sensuous carnival we fear,
Is dead, its pain no longer like a knife
Tapping us on the back. But would our dread
Of nothingness be gone? Not on your life.

August, 2015

   for Carole and Dick

We've met a black, unending wall
Ten miles thick and a hundred high.
This wall's the thought that Dick must die.
We have to meet it; that is all.

Not all. We meet it everywhere,
But it's less dense than we had thought:
There's a lightness beyond – *we're not
All lost.*
         We're gone, and also There.

Are

To think of you,
and you, and you
as "dead" merely
because you've died
belies
your presence – no
mere memory – to me.
You're like the "are"
in "you are dead",
which insists on
shoving the predicate
aside
and standing alone,
alive.

Thinking My Own Death

Death is opaque, disjunct. To think,
I posit Christ as the burning link*
By whom the door through which none see
Becomes a bright transparency.

Afterwards

If after dying we come on again,
It will be not as stars but constellations,
Not single actors but entire casts,
Each of us; everyone we will have been,
Child and adult, will be at one at last,
And join in the familial celebration.

Seventeenth-Century Gravestone for a Child

Chelmsford, Mass.

The Resurrection must take *place*,
As promises take place in deed.
Before the years of rain erase
This slate, finally, let us read
The best these parents can afford,
To claim or tenderly imagine:
Not simply, "She is with the Lord",
But "She is in her Father's mansion".

---

* A torch (archaic)

Antoine

> Dauphin Island, Alabama

Amidst these tombs of solid citizens,
Credentialed tons of stone with fond clichés,
A lichen-crusted wooden cross extends
Its shaft a yard towards heaven. It decays,
And that is true to death. And carved upon
Its arms is mystery – true to life: *Antoine*.

Alzheimer's

With no more blood or pain
Than day becoming night,
The sinews of his brain –
Deep coils of learning, tight,
Compact – are twisted to clots,
Tangles of rotting string.
What held like sailors' knots
Can now hold not a thing.

This, of the ways to die,
Most hurts the askers "why".

Confrontation

"What if this present were [my] world's last night?"
I'd face it with the death-accepting prayer
Of blankness, maybe, of one facing the stare,
Perfectly alien, of a tiger right
In front of him, intent and crouched, right there.
Or try to keep my fate within the scope
Of life, with prayer like lamp whose light is hope.

The Record

Once you're "dead",
you're registered
as having lived.
To most who knew you
you're like a whistle-stop
in Nevada, seen from
the rear of a receding train.
But somewhere –
if you can call it "where" –
I like to think
your whole story's recorded
in perfect language
permanently.

To Andrei Rublev

It's snowing in your church's burnt-out skull;
Blood has frozen to stained glass in the streets;
Tartars, not monks, are at Andronikov.
But you, who neither weep nor curse nor scoff,
You understand, and paint the Trinity.
They have one face. Its mutual gaze meets
Beyond their halos, which are gold but dull,
As if to sharpen the serenity.

Original Stained Glass, North Transept, Reims Cathedral

The suckling Virgin's given God his birth! –
In jeweled windows, blazon of his church;
And this absurdity, believed, will yield
A peace as rich as the glass, as well-annealed.

Notre-Dame de Paris on TV

15 April 2019

Two troughs
of fire, as seen from above,
transepts and nave
forming a cross;
and then
another brilliant cross,
as if suspended
in the nave,
seen through the western portals
and cut by a single
diagonal
slant of sunlight.

A Glass of Benedictine, D.O.M.

As incense colors mysticism,
So does this liquid prism
Refract my mood
To ecstasy:
My self subdued,
I am a monk
Charged with the essence I have drunk.

Going to Aix, Derailed by Taizé

Rejected by Dijon, we stopped to see
The thousand-year-old nave and crypt and courtyard,
Sandstone extravaganza, of Tournus,
Where I, old Baptist, sank down on one knee

And playfully said a prayer
At the thigh-bone of St. Philibert –
Then zap! Leaving the church for Aix, we saw
Across the street an arrow marked "Taizé",
Protestant monastery you'd heard about;
You said "let's go!" We went; and they,
Good monks, accepted the four of us,
Not as apprentice monks,
But in their very own way.

Taizé. Supper at the Reception

The monks ride light on life; they use, don't own.
Tasteful simplicity of wood and stone,
The handmade tables, chairs, and limestone walls,
Enhance the light as evening softly falls.
And Frère Éric presides – or celebrates –
With bread and wine and cheese, on stoneware plates;
His French is like the claret, dry and clear,
As if Rameau were playing his clavier
To set the scene to music. All of this,
For such as me, provides a scent of bliss
Made from this place like scent from an apple tree.
Supper here is another liturgy;
As in their church, it points beyond the cross,
But here it mutes even the thought of loss.

Taizé. The Main Church

After the light and lovely
supper of wine-cheese-bread-and-salad
hosted by Frère Éric for us,
two grownups and two

small children, the tolling
of bells across the way,
heightened by trough of water below,
told us to walk to the Grande Église
for evening service, where,
with organ roaring beauty forth
above, we beheld
some eighty kneeling white-robed monks.
They were like embodied
words for a prayer that we
were almost desperate
to learn.

Beautiful Liturgy, Beautiful Church

– Where is the *cross* in this? Just beauty here!
– Just let that beauty be. What do you fear?

The Life of Prayer

It isn't that God
speaks only
Estonian
or Twi,
so we
can't speak to him;
no, "God always
answers our prayers", you said,
"it's just that we
don't always like
the answers".

Or understand them?
Or even
when breathing
our last, accept them?

Prayer for Continuing Vocation

> after communion

You see me down here, writing
About the faith? I'm flighty,
Given to jags and fads;
So please, don't let this pass.

A Prayer for Fat Souls

Salvation, brave Franciscans, help
Salvage us soldiers of the Cross!
We're crisping in our fat from hell,
Sausages in Satanic pans;
He's walked about the world and found
Whom to devour. But you, with Jesus,
Francis, and seven hundred years
Of fasting – teach us Christian rich
To lose the fat we're frying in!

For Francis Jammes

Angels whose music soothes His anger,
   Play for us;
Saints with a lawyer's gift for language,
   Pray for us;

Donkeys that went to heaven with Francis,
  Bray for us.

Epigrams

1 Lexicography
God is the biggest word. Defined,
Yet not; *God is*, is not *about*;
Shakes the foundation of the mind
When moving into place, or out.

2 It's Time
It's time to learn a word: *God*. If my wit
Can manage. Something might depend on it.

3
Black holes, big bangs, billions of light-years –why
Cavil at meeting Jesus in the sky?

4 The Christian Atheist
Even in formulating cold despair,
He hopes to hurt the God who isn't there.

5
If I abandon *all* for God and die
To self, this lover of God will not be I.

6 2019 AD or AG
"One nation under God" –
Or in these latter days
Of bitter smoke and haze,
Two nations under Gog?

7 Into the Clearing
Dying's like entering a special clearing:
Clinging complexities you leave behind,
For a simplicity you could never find
Because you can't imagine its just appearing.

8 Christian Clichés
They smell like sweetly stale deodorant
To hide the rot of faith no longer meant.

9 Faith
The life of pleasure, rented for a price
At high interest, though palpable as dice
Requires faith that pleasure will suffice.

10 The Ultimate Pun
Two moments – just before, just after we die:
In either place, we're finally *out of time*.

11 Hope: a Theological Virtue
To hope is like imagining,
With final tragedy in sight,
That this one – malgré everything
We know about French novels – might,
For everyone, turn out just right.

12
To have the faith of Francis . . . yes, but how?
Say "I believe". Mean it in deed. And now.

13 The History of Western Philosophy
After the long parade of greatest minds,
Where each, examining the others, finds
Great fault, the hapless student starts to lose
Faith in their thought. Yes – *faith*. "Which do I choose?"

14
Why, after all the blows that strike it,
Or miss (that back-and-forth – immense
Feud of logic and evidence),
Choose Christianity? I like it.

The Incarnation

He loses his temper,
he makes mistakes,
like me
exactly;
but also
shows us something
astounding
(*extonare,* "thundering"),
like an actor
who plays Mr. Darcy
but really is
Mr. Darcy.
What matters here
is the both-at-once,
not appearance and
reality, but two
realities together.

Not the Frontal View

Standing behind the cross, I glimpse,
Through eyes hazed up as if by the wind,
The back of his head – it's lolling down,
A little bloody, somehow crowned;

A hand that dangles limp as a glove;
A bent knee angled out. Enough.

The frontal view is too well known
To see. But here, what barely shows
Is all intimate, like his dying;
And like his rising.

Good Friday. Thinking of Whit

A hard Ignatian exercise:
To feel how nail by nail and gasp
By gasp your savior Jesus dies –
By standing by, trying to grasp
My friend's dying, his nails, his cries.

The Burial of Christ: from the Sterzingen Altarpiece

Two patricians lower his head, his feet,
Both now unmindful of stately beard and gown.
With folds like sculptured marble, the winding-sheet
Conceals their hands, precedes the body down,

Fold over fold, into the oblong tomb.
But Christ, his forearms crossed, is in repose
Above that chasm, light upon its gloom.
His agony, once awesome, only shows

Through dots on hands and feet, and, on his side,
A crescent, brown as rust. His eyes seem closed
In contemplation, as though they had not died;
His features, like his hands, are thin, composed.

The women minister, their eyes downcast.
The churchyard path goes through a gate, then past
Embankments, trees, the hill that bears the Tree,
To a walled medieval town in Germany.

A Question

Who was this man?
I can't understand,
except that he lived
two thousand years ago
and did
strange things, and died for a while,
and that so many've found it
a matter of life and death
to remember him
and do as he said.
Something like
a light
we marvel to look at,
and which also
lights whole tracts
of dark
and drifting fog.

Weight

All of the stones and bricks, in all the churches
In Christendom – so many,
So many – supported by a single person.

Witness

Nobody need believe what I have seen.
Or is it everybody needs to, but
No forcing.
          Open, what had long been shut,
One Easter morning. Out of me he seemed,
This presence right beside me like a beam
Of Person. Saw me wholly, this conscious Light.
Out of myself I seemed, and *it was all right*,
My knowing who he was, his knowing me.

In All Saints Chapel, Sewanee

True, I'd been focused by stained glass and music,
But hadn't come to church to sweetly use it
To churn holy emotions; so, surprised
To find that tears had overwelled my eyes,
Took them at first as signs of unknown sadness.
But then I noticed something slow, then rapid,
Then overwhelming like a coming train,
Yet quiet: *Presence*, like the one in stained
Glass, had revealed itself as here, alive,
And registered in me, right in my eyes.

The Guest

For this distinguished guest, just clean your house.
Luxury's not the business he's about.
Get simple things to eat – some bread, some wine,
Some fish; he likes it broiled from time to time.
All plainness made with fire is to his taste.
He likes your house, and you: look at his face.

Don't entertain him – talk, in your quiet rooms,
For greatest pleasure this side of the tomb.

The Jesus Prayer

Just seven words, nine syllables, repeated
By Greek and Russian Orthodox believers:
"God", the biggest of words, the mystery-chasm
We put ourselves within, not understanding;
"Have mercy", *pitié*, compassion not deserved,
No more than the coming to us of the Word;
"On me", whose face we look at in the mirror,
Uncertain whether to love or hate or fear it;
"A sinner" (is that some of us, or all?),
One who breaks religious or moral law.

"God have mercy on me a sinner." C'est moi.

Poor Woman

Mostly she squats in doorways, hugging knees
Through jeans as meager as the bones beneath,
And taking to and from her sunken mouth
The cigarette that lets her breathing out
In dust-grey clouds that let us see the pressure.
Her feelings build up high. The valve that measures
And checks that danger is her language, running
Out of her mouth in spurts of sullen mumbling,
Unceasing till she hikes her private desert
To yet another doorway.
                      Lady Lizard,
You have a flame that makes this smoky dryness,
And once you threw it at us in defiance –
One night you rose from your slab, and strode, and stalked,

And howled more loudly than we could have thought,
You from whom all but suffering had been stripped,
Not calling Judgment down, but being it.

Worn Thin, and Pierced

All that you know through all your senses – love,
Then coffee, as April morning opens up,
Train-whistles sounding off the hills through fog,
The feel of city tuning up as you walk . . .
And all your thinkings clinging to all that,
Are an opaque, not often noticed wrap
Of lightest film (in times of passions thickest,
But thinning in the night, old age, and sickness)
That covers the nothing, or the everything:
Abyss or Truth, glimpsed when you inward sink
Deep to the consciousness that silence brings.

Breakthrough

Sometimes, my gaze
Will strike so hard
On the hard flat glaze
Cast on my yard
By passing days,
I sharply hear
The crack; and see,
Beneath the veneer,
My willow tree
Glittering clear.

Four Kinds of Celebration

We all have private little celebrations;
We pause from work, say, and sit to a bracing
Pot of coffee with crisply perfect doughnuts,
And think our job may rent but doesn't own us.
And bigger celebrations – barbecues –
Festoon the back yard with the smoke of food
Charred, and splatter the air with spurts of laughter
And popping beercans, all the happy clatter
Of forks and plates. Family and friends, relaxed,
We feel the warm invasion we enact
Of genial spirits mingling with our blood.
And Mardi Gras, the giant feast of love
Of flesh, of hail-farewell to appetite,
Fixed to the Christian year by pagan rites,
Flows through the public places of the town
On tinseled floats with skeletons and clowns –
The people's feast, of fun and fear and money.
But now we have the fiery, flagrant coming
Of fall, for weeks, to all northeastern states.
Who puts it on? What do they celebrate?

Lyric at Dawn

>   Spring Hill, Alabama

When shafts of sun scatter their light
On window panes,
And breakfast on the porch is set
To songbird strains,
And moisture on the flowery leaves
Is iridescent,
It dawns upon us now at last:
This is *our present*.

Photograph of Manhattan, Winter 1887

As vivid as the falling, swirling snow,
These people bustling. "Dust long since", we know.
Reductive! Look – it's *today,* just long ago.

Even As I Walked

   Oxford, England

In Merton Street, on Christmas Eve, it's snowing
In great detail, and Blue Boar Lane is the way
To tea and cakes, and church, late in the day.
Reflecting on this turns my walk to knowing,
Like Middle Ages to medievalism:
Mere accidents, that it is late and snows,
Become *appropriate*, as I compose
The feel of things, the sight, in this revision –
Which even as I walk begins to form –
Of evensong and tea, of walk and storm.

In the Medieval Galleries

The saint in limestone, wooden virgin, chalice
Of gold, glass thick with stain:
Hard vivid *things,* not visions from a palette.

Recipe

Take one fine cluster of associations
And crush them in your mind like Keats's grapes
Till pungency fills your skull, the echo-chamber,

Till you are high on foam of images,
Froth of the past, and flecks of fantasy.
For instance Spring Hill College, where Loyola,
Sculpted, exudes his substance on moody air,
Odor of sanctity and sweat like jasmine,
Pervasive. When I taught there, Jesuit-like,
Hot in a black suit and fervently tending
My German roots and compounds, herbalist
Of words, I thought the plaster in the walkway
Spicy with more than mold. My noontime sandwich,
Its honey squeezed through bread like baklava,
Seemed likewise dense with values. And the church:
On such whiteness of stucco, even shadows
Were bright.   Associations make you drunk,
Yes, but are more complex than grapes, are more
Like okra, shrimp, and rice, the gumbo-stuffs
Of this region that blend when richly mixed –
Like *Jesuit, tropics, incense, work, decay,*
Which make a Catholic summer Spring Hill day.

Churchbells Near Laramie, Long Ago

Bells ring upon the sky like strokes of dawn –
Wide through the air, until entirely gone
Into a silence massive as the day.

Air fresh with light is like an innocence
That any foul mood of ours would betray.
So let's keep cheerful, out of reverence.

Church Downtown

This big-old, shabby, stone, eccentric
Presence, amidst the bored, resentful,
Or hostile people and their boring,
Resentment-building buildings, restores me.
It points, this barely legible sign,
Where friends had sent me; it reminds.

In an Old Cloistered Library

    Oberlin College

It's winter dusk at four;
After a rest, again
The snow is at the pane,
Tentative; on the floor,
It melts from crusted boots.
Deep in my chair, I look
At winter, then my book,
Thinking of old disputes
In Luther's Germany
And Calvin's Switzerland –
Two places that demand
Love for austerity,
For crusty winter, snow,
And dusk.
          This northern cold
Gets to me, fresh yet old;
Logs crackle, settle, glow;
I look beyond the page.
Here is that distant age.

Across from the De Young Museum

Golden Gate Park, S.F.

Even in simple air I watch these pines,
Whose very wood has bent to the demands
Of wind, in shapes that energy defines
And keeps. But now, among the crouching stands

Of pine, air is becoming complicated;
The ocean fog is tumbling massively
Like spirits through the trees – like night created
Suddenly, moist with darkness, from the sea.

This is the Way: I watch yet stay within
The landscape, which is moving, cool, Chinese,
And redolent of where I've always been.
It will suffice, this life of fog and trees.

On Hartmut Thieme's Discovery

So smart, they cut their weighted spears from the *stem*
Of spruce, so long ago
Their trees have turned to coal.

As distant as stars. But God remembers them.

Medieval, and Renaissance Too

Those commonplaces writers spread
Like turds of truth on youthful fires –
"You too, like me, will soon be dead" –
Aren't merely monkish kill-desires.
They're telling the world (in pride!) this truth:
I haven't been deceived by youth.

Resonance

The Middle Ages: hear the resonance?
The somber shaking, ponderous, as of
Foundations thrust through bedrock yet unsteady
Above, where limestone thins to tracery?
It is the frailty of the very stable.
Its middleness is not the Golden Mean,
Nor compromise, nor average, but *between*:
A high, obscure street, with houses impending
On either side, its center line the sharp
Crease of the gutter. Listen – footfalls echo,
Processions coming off the centuries,
As torches flare, fade, and recall the dark.

The Killing of St. Thomas Becket

According to Guernes de Pont-Sainte-Maxence

At last a third blow knocked him down,
Exposed his brain; and Hugo ground
Feet into neck as Thomas writhed.
So braced, he wedged his sword in, pried,
And popped the brain out of the skull
Like meat out of a walnut-shell.
"He'll never come back now – let's go!",
Said Hugo, in his faith, his hope.

Fashions, 1000-2000 AD

Jesus, one thousand, was the Other.
God's Son, but no one's father, brother,
Or husband; on his arms as straight

As cross-beams there's no mortal weight.
His eyes could never move; they stare
Like eggs of punctured stone, to where
Transcendence lurks beyond our sight.
Bernard and Francis set him right,
So that by fifteen-hundred God
Is baby, and his flesh is flawed
Like ours with soft mortality –
From swaddled bundle to corpse on tree,
Stretched out with Dachau scrawniness
From taking burdens that oppress;
No longer very resurrected.

Let's keep transcendence (but corrected).

Randomness

Another 'sixties film: the mannered deeds
Of daring, childlike spontaneity,
With "I dunno", "why not", as all one needs
To give a plot the called-for symmetry –
Of Brownian movement. That's the age's answer
To humanist and Christian woman/man;
Like cell-division modernized to cancer,
Triumphantly. They're doing what they can.

The Dogmatist

There's only one
Way to salvation –
The Interstate,
With franchised stations.
Its many signs
Give one command:

Follow my rules
Or else be damned.

That Old-Time Religion

Join our church, or the God of Love
Will drop you in hell, where, far above,
You'll spy the saints in ecstasy.
(That's to enhance your agony,
Which needs to be complete – the screw,
Twisting, on which you sit, won't do;
Mind, too, must howl! So think: "*Forever*
This pain, and heaven's blisses *never*".)

Surviving Jehovah

That big unstable one who worked us over
With genocide, that ill-formed
Thomas Hardy character called Jehovah –
Angry, vengeful, bloody, almost a joke –
Still left us faith, charity, even hope.

Auctions

Libya has slave
auctions of black
Africans. I heard and
saw one: "700 for him;
eight; going for 800 . . . gone!"
"I need a strong one for
field work . . . "

A Leonardo painting
of Christ, luminously
hypnotic, sold
at auction for nearly
450 million dollars.
Would Christ in person, even more
luminous than his Leonardo
portrait, bring in
450 million dollars?
Not, I think, even
after his Resurrection;
not in the kind of dollars
we deal in.

The Terror

What do we make of this: some forty
thousand guillotined
between September 1793 and
July '94, mostly nobles and
clergy, but others. Not
useful like chickens, which
we eat, but dead on the altar of abstractions,
then to the common pit to rot.
Many a teen-age girl, with "de"
before her name her sin, hauled screaming
thrashing to the heavy reddened blade,
ever more blunt with every neck. No frills and
thrills of first communion and dancing
for these girls. I want to know
how we imagine God forgiving
and loving those perps. Quite
an exercise in theogymnastic
contortions, I suspect.

A Vision of Heaven in the U.S.

Take the standard
schoolroom shooting
of all
the six-year-olds, or random
adolescents,
boiled-down hatred and power
enabled
by the usual AR-15,
re-set it all
the way around,
and we would have
actions of love so
luminous as to
cast into shadow
a mere St. Francis.

Jeremiad for St. Jerome

If you're in heaven, purified
Of all of you that should have died,
One wonders how much could be left.
By choice or temperament bereft
Of love, sex, friendship, honesty,
And courage, you slandered Melanie,
Jovinian – all who disagreed;
Betrayed Rufinus; out of need
To butter up the bishop, twisted
The words of Origen; resisted
The truth with lies and self-denial;
Detested women, all the while
Pressing celibacy on girls

And rich widows. Those strings of pearls
You cast before us married swine:
Eat them and gag, line by pure line.

Little New England Essay in Roughly Metrical Prose

Why do I hate your memory, Cotton Mather? Not just because as child, if one can call it that, you lectured classmates on their sins and wrote them prayers; not just because that childhood blossomed such that the prigs of Harvard reviled you for your priggishness. True, these were signs; and you were one for signs. Was it a mercy-sign that your unpleasant God relieved two wives of your presence by killing them, as he killed thirteen of your children (and made one survivor your financial wrecker and public humiliator), and anesthetized another wife with madness? Your life was one long halloween, all trick no treat, except – prompting an oh so rare usage of "happy" – the witch trials, which you noted in detail, approving the righteous torture and neck-snapping and strangling of women, men, the old, the young; declaring, in a splurge of lawyerly compassion, that if we got the guilty ones, "how happy are we!" No, it's not mainly this I hate you for, old cottonmouth, nor even your prolific prolixity, old blathermather. It's because I, a recent scion of Massachusetts, must, in reading you, experience to its fulsome full this loathsome feeling, hatred, and so must feel my full kinship with you.

Faith, Hope, and Charity

My favorite's Hope.
Faith is like
a body made

by Hope; Charity's
like how that body
behaves.
It's not as though
Faith were a pedestal on which
Hope is mounted, gushing
clear waters of Charity.
No, it's more democratic: you,
and you, and even I, if we
are open to Hope, are
each of us three-in-one, and,
by Hope,
evermore shall bé so.

Eden and After

The light by which we see is one
With the heat by which we live – the sun.
And is the truth sun to our heart?
It was. But they were torn apart
By furies of the old perverse:
"I know the good, follow the worse".

Scripture Lesson

Judas, one of the chosen,
For thirty pieces sold him;
Thomas's faith was pale;
Peter, when tested, failed.
Chosen people are never
Dependable. But devils,
Madmen, the sick, the blind,
Discerned him every time.

The Trinity, Especially the Holy Spirit

"The search for God": as if
for a wallet stiff
with cash but mostly
credit cards – because they bank on faith.
(Unlike mere search for wallet, which takes
only faith that it might be found.)
We might, then, like the Schoolmen, deduce
a God by merest logic,
with cleverest finesse
of propositions; big, then bigger.
This structure we admire. We call it
God. – Jesus we know from scripture:
life story of one of us, lived and died, but
irradiated with divinity. Closer
and closest . . . My favorite is
the Ghost, or, verbally sanitized,
the Spirit. Everyone living has
a spirit, but this one needs
inviting. She's shy. But once
she's in you, she's in. Just listen.

Triads

Sundown Walk in the Sewanee Graveyard, All Saints Day

Low were my eyes, on stones and grief-sweet words;
Then they lifted, to see
Such ambered leaves! Like hallelujahs unheard.

Lazarus

He knew what dying was, having endured it
Twice. But the second time,

As death choked off his breath, he knew securely
What resurrection was: the glorious shouts
Of all he loved, as he obeyed "Come out!"

Tournus. Romanesque Church, ca. 1000 AD

The crypt: its floor assaults my feet with stones
Angled like ill-set teeth.
Not comfortable, down here with God alone.

The Chartres Cathedral

As if, in one élan of sound, a chorus
Of men, women, and angels
Had raised these stones, this glass! just for adoring.

I Read it Somewhere

The rainbow trout has pain-receptors, head
And neck! Can . . . carrots feel?
Empathy rightly spreads its widening net.

At the End of Time

When matter, light, and energy are spent,
God views his work, and says:
"*Done*. But I loved it! Let's begin again . . . "

So Many of Them

Clicking of heels on sidewalk, to St. Margaret's,
Sunday morning. I harkened,
In bed, little Protestant, primly startled.

God and Artists Draw the Line

Let him be spat on, beaten, stripped, and mocked;
Be nailed to a cross; be dead;
But never (swelled-up, wormy, stinking) rot.

The Crucified and the Nothing-Doing

Nailed up to die, gasping – so harsh, unsubtle,
At times I want to flee.
Give me a little Taoist doing nothing.

After Dying

Like flowering into music, if it's joining
With God! If nothing, nothing.
In either case, *we won't be disappointed.*

My People the Portuguese

In Lisbon: Cemetery of the Pleasures,
Whores with names like Mary
Of Jesus . . . In-your-face grotesque. Refreshing.

A Consideration

She's gone from you forever, with her talk
And touch?
              True; but forever
Is made of time. Where she has gone is not.

In All Saints Chapel, Sewanee

These intervals – of Bach, of windows – arrange
The movement of my feelings.
Such onward ecstasy these forms contain!

Pope John Paul II, Easter 2001

Bent at right angle, mumbling to God – none better,
But for Jesus, to show us:
As to suffering, we're in this together.

Are We

Are we, as bags of chemicals, like lamps
Whose workings make the light?
Or are we light itself, unshaped, unspanned?

Advent, Taizé

Singly, then all at once, from bell-tongues issue
Ringing cascades of clangs
And under-boomings. "Come!" Who could not listen?

Francisco de Oliveira and Margarida de Jesus

    São Miguel, Açores

A faint page in the Archives; rainy stones
That slant like longhand – these
Their monuments, the Book of Life their hope.

Azorean Church

Babies as angels wriggling, Mother rapt –
No otherworldly faith,
Just eyes upcast and Jesus pink and fat.

The Crucifixion and the Holy Spirit

"Then he gave a great cry, and breathed his last."

The breath outlived the cry.
But both we yet can hear – the God, the man.

Figurines in a Sunday School Sandbox

A baby, on a donkey like that other;
Here bound for Egypt, later for the cross.
I wished they'd given him a blanket-toss,
Maybe, not crucifixion.
                          Here his mother,
Donkey, and father – towards a future seen
In retrospect and from eternity –
Traverse a desert.
                    What this meant to me
Was sand through fingers: soft-hard, soothing, clean.

Membership

At eight I founded a society
Of "devils". Throwing darts into the spine
Of what our church had given me as sign –
The Bible – of the love that sets us free,
And my accepting Jesus, was our rite.
What made me pierce that gilt/black spinal cord
Like a mosquito, aping those who bored,
With lance, his side? Some anti-mama spite?
A biting, itchy need for saving face
With boys who lightly sneered at Jesus-stuff?
Just foolish child's aggression; but enough
To punch my ticket to the human race.

Baptism at Twelve

I got beyond the old men honking hymns
Caruso, even, couldn't have beautified,
And past the preacher's whisper-then-howl that dims
All light but hell's, because I had to decide,

And did. I had him dunk me in the tank –
No sprinkle, this, no touch of wet, genteel
And adequate. I couldn't say I stank,
Then came up clean of sin; I didn't feel,
Except the water; didn't think; I saw
The people looking at me just before,
And then just after. But as sinking raw
And rising cooked will change your status – more,
Your worth – so by his change from *once* . . . to *then* . . .
Just that, this shrimp was never the same again.

A Collegiate Leavetaking

Hopeful wiseguy, I tried the Quakers; sniggered
At bellyrumblings – the Inner Voice, I figured.
Tried a nice church: too bland for holy mysteries.
It tasted like a bowl of Jeezes Kristies.
But no, I wasn't searching deeply, advancing
Along the pilgrim's footpath; I was dancing,
To rhythms banging through my blood and flesh,
Driving me where I yearned to merge or mesh –
With girls, with verse. So on I jigged with joy,
The sipping, sampling, drifting, dancing-boy.
Fourth year, a private course on Christian mystics;
We gauged their depth with academic dipsticks,
And I was not to grope for God. I didn't.
So much, I thought, for searching, and good riddance:
> *Much to be done,*
> *Under the sun,*
> *That's much more fun.*

At the Wide Gate

1
I'll tell you what I am:
Salty as Smithfield ham,
And hardened just as well
By the slow smokes of hell.

2
The embassy that Satan made in me
Is well kept up, although I broke relations,
Formally, long ago. My protestations,
They say, are just formal; they'll wait and see.

3
Can thought alone compel
Thy peace? It is no use.
It brings me to a hell
As cold as self-abuse.

Christian Heritage

Who is in charge? "Bear this or break –
No bending: *always will what's best*".
This is a will that I contest.
My self-possession is at stake.

Radical Delight

Who *are* you?   Why do you not let me live
As I please?   And how could your caress, so rough,
Be kinder than my smooth alternative?

Your steel-brush strokes are forcing me to slough,
Daily, my fleshy growths of appetite,
But still they come; I cannot have enough.

I would forever scratch my itches, light
At first, then harder at the thickened sore;
But you would give me radical delight,
Gouging my itches till I have no more.

Confirmation

Lost in a state of soul and mind and spirit
As brooding as the fog on San Francisco;
As shifty as the shreds of fog in trees;
As dark as fog when fog alone can be seen –
I struck a word that flared: *unnecessary*.
No need to grope through air where light is buried!
Look! You have legs; they move. Get out of here!
It's clarity you want? Go where it's clear.

On the Right Surface

For many years I went to eucharist
In hope of making God for me exist.
Those words repeated, and the wine and bread,
Could make me sure of rising from the dead
If they would just pervade my soul, as wine
Pervades the blood. Ingesting the divine,
I would assimilate myself to God.
It was a flawless plan; but I was flawed.
Each Sunday felt like the unlively scratch –
On the right surface – of a fogdamp match:
Enduring surface, match still unconverted
To flame. For years. And then one day, it spurted.

Sunday

Like bookends from the library of time,
A vice presses last Sunday to the next,
Tighter each week, tight as a perfect rhyme.
Not Saturday to Saturday, or even
Weekend to weekend, let alone some day
Or other, only Sunday. Yet in youth,
I thought of Sunday as just no-time-for-play,
Stuffy Sunday; dreary radio-music
To set boiled dinner stuffing my stomach. No,
No pleasure, but no school, later no work,
And always church patiently lurking, though
I paid no mind.
              So time keeps lapsing faster;
But more and more steadily, weekdays keep
Collapsing into a Sunday dense and deep.

Anyday Drama

For the shadow of
an instant
I felt myself to be
perfectly beatific, like
a freshly minted angel. Then
the mortal-moral black
screen shuts down
again,
and here
I am.

The Little Things

The acrid cellar-smell of swept garage,
Heavy and hot and musty, caught me sweetly;
In novel counterpoint, prepared my nostrils
For scent of pine-sap so intense – the door's
Now opened – that it seems the gist of green,
There in the back where I'd been laying bare
The trunks of trees in the woods of Tennessee
Behind our house. Then out front on the driveway:
Gravel in chunks. My shoes can't rustle it,
Nor can the loudest rivulets from downpours.

These are . . . the data for an argument?
Incitements? Promptings? Lightnesses of being?
These are my angels, messengers from elsewhere,
Whose instruments have strings that sing within,
On the same frequency in me, in them,
An insight startling with simplicity :
What's been enacted is beatitude.

Prayer for Himself

The child I was, gone but not dead,
Lives in this dome of heaven – my head.
In retrospect I cherish him
Who at the time could never shed
Self-loathing, as one sheds a skin.
May God, who keeps what is alive,
And leaves as cast-off flesh our sin,
Cherish me thus when I arrive.

The Indwelling Spirit

It is a shaft of light,
This axis of the mind,
Which my corrosive hate,
My lusts of touch and sight
And all our rot combined
Can never penetrate.

"Credo Quia Absurdum"*

When casually
a TV celebrity
said "I don't believe in God" –
the one spelled out in the Bible – I
felt sad. But why
should such remarks, opinions, caught on the fly,
matter? Could it be
that I, by choosing to
be Baptist-baptised in a tank at twelve,
and Anglican-confirmed at twenty-six,
showed that I loved that heady stuff, and wished
everyone else could love it too?
Absurd; but there you are.
Christianity's
on best of terms
with the absurd.

---

* "I believe because it is absurd"
      ? Tertullian

August 16, Church of the Reconciliation, Taizé

"There were no blocks of straw", said Brother Roger,
"That was at Christmas, this is Assumption-tide."

But what I'd seen, I'd seen: black figure leaning
Downward, as though in static focus, over
A perfect little disc of light that blackness –
Of robe and wimple – highlights in the straw,
The blocks and blocks of straw!
                                    I tapped your arm,
You looked, and didn't see it: what I took,
At first, for playful work of ceiling-lights.
(There were no lights.)
                      Later, it came to mind
That I'd been much in debt to mothers, marriage . . .
Women; I'd variously infringed – like surf
That feeds itself at the expense of beach.
And I was given this. It gave me pause

True Desire

>" . . . attempts to eat beauty, to eat
>what we should only look at"
>
>   —Simone Weil

When I behold the way you're meant to be –
You're looking up, with smile live as your eyes,
Making your mood as clear as ABC –
I want to take you in; metabolize,

Not understand; not read you right, but *eat*.
My little love-chicken of spicy flavor,
I would roast you in my oven heat!
Then, like a special wolf who's learned to savor,

I'd slowly, bones and all, make you my own.
Pallid romantics, pressing soul to soul,
Or even rubbing flesh, making sweet moan –
What do they know of true desire's goal,

Absorption of the One, assimilation? . . .
Come here. I feel that certain need for you
That sets me whetting towards a consummation
Only communion-eaters might construe.

A Wedding

Spring Hill, Alabama

Old church, old music, Book of Common Prayer,
And we were married new that August day.
The whole tradition, like the heavy air,
Bore down; but we could take it any way,
Within the bounds of reason. ("If these bounds
Are crossed, your one flesh may be cut in two.")

Old words, dense as the air, have been the grounds
On which we stand, substance of all we do
In Reason's realm, where we were married true.

Afterlife for a Couple: Two Takes

1
Belovèd, we have shed the clinging mist
Of thoughts and things and persons that exist;
Of all the life we had – no ash, no spark.

Yet you are here, beside me in the dark.

2

Where is the fleetingness of *now*? We stay
In this enlightened place the livelong day,
Forgetting time and death – they had to die,
And we are here together, you and I.

Compline

I shape this day till I can feel its heft,
Distributing each major stress and weight
Rhythmically, harmonizing what is left,

Until its form and burden, however great,
Sit lightly in my comprehension's palm –
My property and handiwork, not freight.

My good, my bad, in the senescent calm
Of evening come to terms. I contemplate
And weigh them now, like phrases of a psalm.

Halloween by San Francisco Bay

Either the sky's so hard a blue a shout
Could echo off it, chipping flakes from brilliant
Air, or the sea-fog folds its phantoms over,
And closes us in mystery cool from afar.
It is the time for change to come upon us.

I've watched our children year by year with joy
Enter into this season; now they're leaving.
No more excitement as night clamps down at six,
Brisk with its scent of cider and adventure.
They leave, but I now enter Hallows' Eve
While jack-o-lanterns flare, the moon glares down,

And children mark a distance with their fading
Shouts in the dark. O luminous emblems, skulls
And souls, all souls, I celebrate your coming.

Christmas Eve

From the high altar, gospel words descend
Like pebbles that the world's snarled currents bend,
Slow, and distract from falling free.
But I can wait here patiently;
For here, at bottom, all that falls must end,
Before it rises like the mustard-tree.

Outside Benson, Arizona

An arch of white reindeer, and manger scene
With many donkeys, in styrofoam and clean,
Stand up across a sand-hot mangy yard,
In front of the worn-down house. Here life is hard,
We see, but they will keep their Christmas just
The same. So what if Christmas snow is dust.

Christmas

It's Christmas morning yet again; the birth
Of Jesus, to be marked with holy mirth.
We know of course it's Wholly Money Day,
Provoking weeks of shopping; we glut and pay.

Yet nothing's changed. Inquisition, Crusade –
Scars on the Body of Christ that never fade.
Yes, we are all in this together, hell's

Angels like apes and pigs with Christmas bells.
Meanwhile the churches ring their message out,
Rejecting our indifferentness and doubt.

New Year's Eve, and the Millennium's

I think of Thomas Hardy, perched
On the fence between his century
And mine; the truth for which he'd searched,
In youth, become an effigy
Of horror, God as Imbecile;
Not searching now, unhappy still.

But then that "àged thrush, with blast-
Beruffled plume", sang him a song
Obscure with "blessèd hope". – At last,
It's New Year's Eve; it's been a long
Millennium. Its contents spill
Into the next, which they will fill,

A bit, for most; much more for me . . .
The countdown's started; by the second,
As though for some explosion. I see,
Clearly at last, how life is reckoned:
In moments, ticking down the slope –
Or upwards, each a holder of hope.

Easter Vigil at St. Mark's

Voskresénia! Resurrection!
"Chríst is rísen fróm the déad
trámp-ling dówn déath by déath
ánd upón those ín the tómbs
bestów-ing lífe!"

Over and over, faster
and faster, more and more and
louder and louder
stressed by the stamping
trampling feet of the con-
gregation, this
is the sound of Resurrection.

www.ingramcontent.com/pod-product-compliance
Lightning Source LLC
Chambersburg PA
CBHW061506040426
42450CB00008B/1503